Puffin 1

birds beast

William Hart-Smith was born in England, raised in New Zealand, and spent most of his career in Australia. He produced perhaps a thousand poems in his life. His work was noted, on the one hand, for its clarity and simplicity and, on the other hand, for its capacity for wonder and insight into natural things, the connections among them, and their relationships with us. For decades now his work has been popular in schools and it has been widely anthologised in poetry books for children in Australia and overseas. His poems are children's poems in the sense that they can be appreciated by children in primary as well as secondary schools.

'William Hart-Smith opens our eyes to what is around us, which is the most important function a poet can perform and one which is needed now as never before.'

Moira Robinson

birds
beasts
flowers

Australian children's poetry by

William Hart-Smith
Edited by Brian Dibble

Puffin Books

Puffin Books
Penguin Books Australia Ltd
487 Maroondah Highway, PO Box 257
Ringwood, Victoria 3134, Australia
Penguin Books Ltd
Harmondsworth, Middlesex, England
Viking Penguin, A Division of Penguin Books USA Inc.
375 Hudson Street, New York, New York 10014, USA
Penguin Books Canada Limited
10 Alcorn Avenue, Toronto, Ontario, Canada M4V 3B2
Penguin Books (N.Z.) Ltd
182-190 Wairau Road, Auckland 10, New Zealand

First published by Penguin Books Australia, 1996
1 3 5 7 9 10 8 6 4 2
Copyright © William Hart-Smith, 1996
Copyright in this Collection © Brian Dibble, 1996

Typeset in 13/19 Perpetua
Made and printed in Australia by Australian Print Group,
Maryborough, Victoria

National Library of Australia
Cataloguing-in-Publication data:
Hart-Smith, William, 1911–1990.
Birds, beasts, flowers – : poems
Includes index.
ISBN 0 14 037724 7.
1. Natural history – Australia – Juvenile poetry.
2. Children's poetry, Australian. I. Title.
A821.3

For William Hart-Smith's grandchildren:
Fiona, Gene, Jennifer, Kate, Kathleen, Laura, Mark,
Nicholas, Osmanthus and Warwick

To

Claire

Merry Christmas

from
Uncle George

& Toll
xx

Foreword

William Hart-Smith, who was born in 1911 and who died on Easter Sunday in 1990, is a poet who sees clearly and speaks simply. He perceives things in detail and then represents them vividly, almost as if speaking on behalf of the world itself, a philosophy summed up in his poem 'Preamble':

> Give back to things
> what they already have.

A blackboy wears a charcoal overcoat, a blown-over butterfly rights itself like a yacht, a candle licks the black fur of a room – such images help us to see nature anew and to make fresh meanings there.

We chose the title *Birds Beasts Flowers* for two reasons. First, although Bill left school early, he was very well read, being converted to poetry through his chance discovery of D. H. Lawrence's remarkable book of poems *Birds, Beasts and Flowers* in the Auckland Public Library in the 1930s. Secondly, the title points to the world that most interested Bill and about which his poems see/say so effortlessly but compellingly: he shows us a bird whose cawing flight scores a line across the almost-completed sunset watercolour, or he presents leaves as 'ink-ghosts on the pure white paper of space'. That is, he speaks always from an intimate knowledge of nature — he was a keen fisherman throughout his life and a shell collector when older, as one might guess from reading 'Limpets' — in fact, a species of cowry he discovered was named after him.

Bill Hart-Smith called himself an 'Australasian' poet, a reasonable claim since he spent about an equal number of years in New Zealand and Australia from 1936 onwards, creating precise and memorable images of both countries in his many volumes of poetry. Here we have collected together poems which make us see Australian birds, beasts, flowers and landscapes from arresting angles. By experiencing Hart-Smith's world, we might all be encouraged to give back to our own world what it needs. That would be the greatest tribute we could pay to this unusual and too-little-known poet.

Brian Dibble
Professor of Comparative Literature
Curtin University

Contents

Birds

Bellbirds	3
Fly-catcher	3
Cormorants, Trigg Island	4
Crow	5
Sparrow Hawk	5
Eaglehawk	6
Enough's Enough	8
Divergence	10
Pigeons	11
Follow My Leader	12
Galahs	13
Heron	14
Kookaburras – Kalamunda	16
Night-singing Bird	17
Silver-eyes	18
Bellbirds and a Thrush	20

Beasts

Butterfly (1)	23
Ants	24

Crickets	25
Spider	26
Triantelope	27
Sand Crabs	28
Limpets	29
Blue-bottles	30
Jellyfish	31
Razor Fish	32
Salmon	33
Shark	34
Neptune's Horses	36
Horse in the Rain	37
Relativity	38
Hare	40
Kangaroos	42
Lizard	44
Blue-tongue	45
Two Lizards	46
Butterfly (2)	48
A Poet Farms	50
Flowers	
Leaves (1)	53
Blackboy	54

Puffballs   55

The Coming of the Flowers   56

Trigger-plants   57

Kangaroo Paw   58

Trees are the World's Lungs   59

Syllable Count Poem (1)   60

Citriodora   61

Paperbarks   62

Pillow Poem (2)   63

Camphor Laurel   64

Pines   65

Blackboys in Flower   66

Leaves (2)   67

Landscapes

Dawn   71

Morning Over Perth   72

Early Morning   73

Pattern on a Pavement   74

The Beach   75

Shell-collecting   76

Entente Cordiale   77

The Dam   78

Lake Monger   79

Vapour Trail	80
Thunderstorm	82
Welshpool Road	83
Smoke on the Plains	84
Burning Off	85
Looking for Shells	86
Night Fishing	87
Mini Poem from a Pillow	88
Full Moon	89
Candle	90
Derelict House	91
Kumara	92
Tractor	93
Haystacks and Limestone	94
Windmill	95
Lighthouses	96
Cyclone	100
The Ghost of MacKenzie's Dog	102
Can You Stand Still Enough . . . ?	104
Derelict Hut	105
Full Moon (1)	106

birds

Bellbirds

Bellbirds chiming in the bush
while the ice-cubes clink,
clink, in my glass of orange-juice.

Fly-catcher

The way the Fly-catcher
darts from the Flame-tree in the carpark
to snatch a fly
close to my ear

reminds me of my mother
crocheting.

Cormorants, Trigg Island

Fourteen white-fronted shags
like bits of Chinese ideograms
are perched on a jagged lump of limestone rock
above me as I turn the seaweed over for shells
brushing the flies away
and the sand-hoppers.

I like the way they accept the fact
I'm about some business of my own
that neither concerns them nor threatens.
We live as live-and-let-live things.
I gather shells.
They dry their wings.

Crow

With a single caw
of unutterable despair
a black crow
scored a line of charcoal
right across this almost-completed
sunset watercolour.

Sparrow Hawk

High above the screen
of the Lakeway Drive-in at sundown
a motionless hawk
is a midge
lodged in the fluid
of the sky's bloodshot eye.

Eaglehawk

Eaglehawk is like a leaf in the air
All day long going round and round in circles,
Sometimes dark against the sky
And sometimes with his great wings tipped
    with light
As the sunset edges the clouds . . .
Only when night comes and the fire-beetle stars
Twinkle overhead,
Is the sky empty of Eaglehawk.

Eaglehawk sees all the world stretched out
    below,
The animals scurrying across the plain
Among the tufts of prickly porcupine grass,
Valleys to the east and plains to the west,
And river-courses scribbled across the desert
Like insect tracks in sand; and mountains
Where the world sweeps up to meet him and
    falls away.

The animals live in the dust,
But Eaglehawk lives in the air.
He laughs to see them.
And when the pans dry up and the rivers
    shrink,
He laughs still more, and laughing
Sweeps half across the world to drop and drink.

Enough's Enough

Magpies aren't greedy
birds like seagulls which
have an inexhaustible
appetite
and squabble among themselves
a sight to see them
catch their food in flight

No, they lope
they run
to my outstretched hand
with the bit
of raw red meat held out in it
and accurately snatch it

Beak is the equivalent
of finger and thumb
but more selective
less acquisitive
a most efficient instrument
nevertheless

When the Magpies come
planing gliding
down from the gum
four or five
and sometimes six of them

they betray a kind of
oblique concern
for one another
retire and let each other have a turn.

Divergence

One obstinate gull
prefers to point his tail
into the wind, just to be different
perhaps. Not like all the other chaps.

Wind sleeks skull
and shoulder feathers where they all
stand expectant on the sand. Ruffles his. As each
holds his ground, tufts him along the beach.

Pigeons

The flock of pigeons
that went across the harbour
like a salvo of shells
aimed at the Military Barracks
has perfected the image
by reappearing for a moment
over the distant roofs
in a burst of minute sunlit fragments.

Follow my leader

A flight of white   pigeons
a shoal of birds

goes wheeling over suburban roofs
in the evening light   round

and round and round
over the tranquil chimney smoke

Follow my leader   On the turn
Who's turn?

Who is the leader of the flock?

Galahs

There are about fifty of them
on the stony ground,

some standing still,
some moving about.

Nothing much of pink
breast or lighter-hued crest

shows in the twilight
among the stones.

They are standing about
like little grey-coated aldermen

talking in undertones.

Heron

A grey heron in the twilight
is flying over the tree-tops.

His legs trail behind him like thin straws
and his neck is double-curved like the letter S.

His beak is a radar needle pointing him home.
He is making for the reservoir in the hills

and must get there before nightfall,
his roosting-place where he sleeps standing.

Before I wake tomorrow morning
he will have flown over the trees again

out over the plain towards the city
and the lake in the park there

where he will tread his own reflections
and prick the water with his pointed stick,

lift and put his feet into the water
without the slightest disturbance

for all the world like a sleeper rising early
and stepping into his trousers.

Kookaburras — Kalamunda

From a machine-gun nest
in a gum-tree
at the edge of the escarpment

six guns opened fire at once
belts chattering
barrels running red hot

following an exploratory burst
a chuckle of tracers
sent downhill by a wakeful sentry

at something he saw
moving
up the slope in the twilight
among the boulders of red granite

Night-singing Bird

I wonder whether the magpie
who throat-whistled melodiously
far away in the night last night
was a fledgling still learning
who woke up too soon
and got night and day mixed up
because of a very bright full moon

Silver-eyes

Birds
falling like raindrops

small   silent
olivegreen birds

birds with white rings
around their eyes

Silver-eyes
on a cloudless March morning

are raining drop by drop
into the garden

and all's so   still

Here and there a thin
high
branch of a sapling   bends
with the weight of a bird

like a raindrop
that drops to a lower twig

The Silky-oak too
is taking a small bird-rain

in scattered drops that fall
to the ground and stir the grasses

Then all goes again
suddenly still

when the shower
the bird-shower passes

Bellbirds and a Thrush

Now the cyclorama of night is softly
warmed with daylight and the
stars go out the glow-worm stars go out
in the sky and underneath the fern.
The first chimes of dawn are struck
in the trees' darkening silhouette.
It is as if the birds themselves provide
the first chirrup only and the three
ascending chimes are bells hung in the trees,
a thousand bells, a thousand thousand bells,
until the moment when the sun appears:
they dematerialise: now in the hush
the welcome of a solitary thrush.

beasts

Butterfly (1)

Whenever I peep
over the shoulder of a butterfly
to see what she's reading

she shuts the book.

Ants

In this forty-degree heat
when each bit of raw, red meat
I flick to a pair of magpies
begging for something to eat
sticks to the concrete,
how is it the ants can stand it
scribbling excitedly about so
on their little bare feet?

Crickets

She said what kind of bird is that
singing in the night?

I said it was no bird
but a cricket

bubbling in a tuft of weed
under a street-light.

And many more we heard
positioned about.

With them it may be such
that what we hear

as sound
they feel as touch.

Spider

Not for the spider
To hold the design
Of his delicate web
In his vision, as mine.

Not for him pattern
Of spiral and spoke,
Only a nebulous
Silvery smoke.

Fit for his purpose,
Blindly he weaves
With the sap of his body
A home in the leaves.

Triantelope

When I switched on the bar-light
in the bathroom after midnight —

above the basin, on the wall
a black glove, a furry gauntlet —

the shock made my scalp tingle
and my icy flesh creep.

I cried out,
but remembered

that the house was asleep.
I slippered back to bed

along the dark hall,
avoiding the table,

the chairs,
not touching the wall.

Sand Crabs

Why do sand crabs witlessly
advertise their boltholes
burrows
on the unblemished sand
with an asterisk of pellets?

Limpets

Down there on the dark rock sharp to the foot,
browsing on greenstuff as the cattle do,
the limpets,
whose houses are little pyramids of stone.

Deep in the press of the tide in the dim light
where the to-fro drag of the waves moves the
weed-fronds
whose tips describe their endless sensuous
curves,
very like tanks and other armoured machines,
the limpets deploy.

Now who would ever believe,
seeing these creatures when the water is gone,
clamped fast, fixed rigid,
or cementing themselves at a touch,
they lift their skirts and dance a slow pavan
when the cold green water replaces the hostile
sun?

Blue-bottles

Someone is flying balloons
in the sea, and letting them go.
Little blue-bag balloons
with long trailing strings that sting
the white hands of earth-children.
Children of mermen and mermaids
are flying balloons
in the sea far below
and letting them go.

Jellyfish

Jellyfish are sea bells
bells in the sea
adrift from the towers
of drowned carillons

A pure gelatinous sensuality

Hearts that continue to beat
when all the blood's drained out

The sun casts the shadow
of their long tentacle strings
on the sand
in the clear shallows

Jellyfish are bells
with undulating rims
sea bells
bells in the sea

ringing inaudible requiems.

Razor Fish

If you were
to draw
lightly
a straight line
right
down
the margin
of this
sheet of
paper
with your
pen
it wouldn't be
as thin
as a
Razor Fish
seen
edge
ways
on

If you were
to cut
the shape
of a
fish
out of transparent
cellophane
with a
tiny
tail fin
and a mouth
as long
and sharp
as
a
pin
and let it drift
tail up
head down
you wouldn't see –

the Razor Fish
See
what
I
mean?

Salmon

Wouldn't you think the salmon
would come into the river from the sea
with the weight of the sea behind them pouring in
to fill the wide wings of the lagoon?
Instead, when the tide runs out,
the black and pointed fins
of the salmon fish that wait
move in and close into a flood
of tumbling water yellow-white with mud.

Shark

If the shark is my enemy
I am his enemy too.

There are circumstances I can think of
When I would express my hate

and destroy him. But today
when we skimmed over him,

circled, scratching the roof of his world,
shaking loose the tiles of sunlight,

there was peace between us: a truce.
He did not move. He stayed,

shadow and substance fused,
buoyant in mid-water below us.

Evolution perfected him
a hundred million years ago,

sharpened his snout and honed his teeth,
finishing him excellently. To him

we are only a temporary phenomenon
he leaves to our own devices.

Neptune's Horses

Under the sea, deep
on the ocean floor,
are their stables
and the drowned

fields where they pasture
on weed green and red
or lift their necks
to crop the trees of kelp.

Sometimes they rise
when the great gales
howl and blow,
break to the surface

whinnying, tossing
the hair of their manes
and unkempt
tails. They kick

with mighty shuddering kick
our helpless ship.

Horse in the Rain

A golden stallion with honey-coloured mane
alone in the paddock
celebrates the rain.

He canters around the parched
field as if it were a circus ring,
dust steaming from his hooves.

His sides are streaked and his back stained dark,
his neck a fountain streaming hair,
his tail is curved like a question mark.

Relativity

The main reason why dogs
love to sit in cars
is because
when a dog's inside
a car doesn't move.

When the doors
of the small intimate room
with master and mistress in it
close

the room bucks
and barks and makes
most unusual noises
and odours

then houses get up and run
trees get up and run
posts get up and run
and telegraph poles

in fact everything does

With his nose thrust out
bang in the eye of the galloping wind
his right ear streaming
like a strip of rag in a gale

he for a change can sit still
chin on the window-sill

and let the world do all the running about.

Hare

He comes loping across the flat from the direction of
 the willows.
He is reddish-brown in colour and small indeed from
 this distance.
The white sheep are still, or moving forward slowly
 as they graze,
and the white lambs are lying down by the side of the
 sheep.
And the hare comes skipping across my line of vision,
 thinking I do not see him.
And I would not have seen him had he not moved.
He stops behind a tuft of tussock and lifts his ears
 and his head and his nose,
and I can see him, I can see his ears.
I could shoot him from here with a single shot through
 the tussock;

but I have no gun.

He moves again, boldly across the open; not running,

advancing from cover to cover and stalking the house that

       sits on the hill

and watches the fields and hills,

and the river and the trees,

the still white sheep and the still white lambs.

He thinks the house is a face that watches the world on

       a sharp look out for hares,

with its doorway mouth and window eyes that shine in

       the sun,

and the roof for a large red hat and the chimney a gun.

Kangaroos

Brown out of the brown tussock a darker brown
head rises as if thrust up cautiously on a pole.

A green bird on a feathering grass-stem,
that bends under its weight, flutters

and sinks out of sight. It is the only disturbance
except for the reiterated clicking of castanets

and the fife-notes of insects.

One notices the head gone,
pulled down out of sight, like the vanished bird,

but all over the unfurled
map of the landscape minute brown

figures, dots, jump, all diminishing, yet
each pursuing

lines that intersect, making a maze
of crazy map-lines, meaningless angles.

The skin of the land is a deep fur
maddeningly come alive

with deliberate great fleas.

Lizard

Yes, I'll stop for a snake
and let him pass
across the highway
to the roadside grass,

pull up and let a Blue-tongue go,
at a half-a-mile-an-hour or so
to safety;
and do it again and again, although

the last I saved from certain death
hissed and turned his blue-stained mouth
and clamped it on my toe.

.

Blue-tongue

A yellow lizard
going across the road
from one side
to the other
has been run over

Even lizards bleed
red blood

Like a lost shoe
kicked aside
when dead

Shoes die too.

Two Lizards

A quickly drying trail
of water-drops on the hot
sandstone shelf

from the brink
of a pool
of tannin-stained

rain-water
was made by the tail
of a lizard

come out from the grass
to drink.
I did not see it,

simply knew
that a black twig
by a seepage-pool

had suddenly
flicked from view.
Another lizard froze

on the edge of the sky
where a mat of dodder vine
had netted a hedge.

His very immobility
I think
was what made him conspicuous.

We stopped and stared,
We froze ourselves.
He didn't even blink.

Butterfly (2)

Injured, it walked on my finger.
Wind blew it over.
Came upright again
like a yacht.

Held my hand out
so as not
to damage its wings
any more than they were

with butterfly-living's
wear and tear
and of its one-day life
getting near.

And walked it off
on to a rose.
It walked on its face.
A better place

to expire I thought
than a street where cars
and people pass.
What funny things one does.

A Poet Farms

Kneel and feel with your hands,
your palms, the ground,
the grass where the cow was.
How warm it is!
She has ironed the place
where she was lying
with the press of her body,
the coverlet of Capeweed, Clover,
Paterson's Curse.
Early in the morning,
where she lay all night,
sometimes the ground when she gets up,
visibly steams.

flowers

Leaves (1)

First come the blunt
sticky buds

blots of green ink

and then the paper is folded,
invisible fingers press

and leaves form

Ink-ghosts
on the pure white paper of space.

Blackboy

Fire can't take me by the throat.
I wear a charcoal overcoat.

Puffballs

After the rain
some creamy-white

puffballs
ballooned on the lawn overnight.

I thought my son
had left some of his toys out.

The Coming of the Flowers

They had all time in front of them.
That's why there was no haste.
There was any amount of space too,
a vast waiting wilderness, a waste

which they could people with themselves,
so curiously stirring with new powers;
settle unobtrusively among ferns, cycads, pines
and quietly experiment with flowers.

Trigger-plants

Trigger-plants have their hammers pulled back
full cock, and the safety-catch is off. Their
pans are primed with pollen powder. Trigger-plants,
flowers of many colours, in racemes and spikes, singly
or massed like pin-cushions, every flower a face
aiming a gun at nothing in particular. They are
hair-triggered and when they go
off you don't hear a sound.

Kangaroo Paw

A Kangaroo Paw
by the roadside

with scarlet trousers

is thumbing a lift
with a vivid green thumb.

Trees are the World's Lungs

Trees are the world's lungs, gills.
They take all day to take

one deep breath, and all night long
to exhale. The steady pulse

of their blood
is the flow of sap

seeping through the membrane walls
of cells,

coming down,
and rising up.

Syllable Count Poem (1)

It saddens me to see the fallen trees
all felled and rolled and tumbled into heaps
ready for burning: cadavers, corpses
left on a battlefield. Now softly weeps
a thin and melancholy rain from clouds
that drift in low over this once proud hill.

Citriodora

The tall slender gum
on the lawn by the red brick church
is leisurely dusting its tiles
with a feather duster.

Paperbarks

Clusters of Paperbark trees
left at random in these fields cleared for pasture
and standing in isolated groups
remind me of conspirators planning revolution,
heads together,
arms on each other's shoulders.

Pillow Poem (2)

I'm looking forward to Spring again already

when the wattle trees put on their yellow gloves

and over the long
grey-green sleeves of their leaves

pull gauntlets of yellow fur

right up to the elbows.

Camphor Laurel

The enormous cumulus
cloudlike mass of foliage
of the Camphor Laurel
trees even on the stillest of days
is never still.
Perpetually boiling
it seems to be
to keep itself cool.

Pines

Cones exploding sharply in the heat? . . .

and I thought it was the voice of branches
talking when they meet.

Strange flowers these,
that bloom woodenly in dark trees
and open their petals in audible jerks.

But that's evidently the way
a pine tree works.

Blackboys in Flower

All up the hillside
like so many surveyors' rods
marking something or other at random;
and it was a hot burn last year.

The fire burned three nights,
killing some of the trees.
A stump here and there
smouldered on sullenly,
a red oven underneath,
for a week after.

And now, this miracle,
this upward thrust
of stubborn, straight rods. Phalloi.
Pure upright, perfect perpendiculars,
starred with flowers,
flowered with stars.

Leaves (2)

Leaves are cold green
eyes
looking for light

Leaves are tongues
lapping light
from a blue saucer

Leaves
are fingertips
touching the stream of moving air

testing the temperature.
Leaves can hear
they listen for the rain

and other things as well
Leaves
have a sense of smell . . .

landscapes

Dawn

Wading into the warm sea
to wash my feet

The agony of cold sand
There I found

an all-night fisherman
sitting on his three-spiked stool

had hooked the sun
and was slowly reeling it in.

Morning Over Perth

A single cloud over the city
at first light this morning

heavily bellied with rain

High up under it   an eagle
small   a black speck

circling slowly

reminds me of a ship

the bird a pilot
come to guide her in.

Early Morning

Here on the side of a hill
stand still   quite still
and listen   will you?
to the sound of raindrops falling

to the ground   behind you
and all around
on the face   and hands
drops gathered   garnered

by the surface of leaves
of sapling   and shrub   and trees
with their crowns high
and out of sight

falling through a drift
of cottonwool   mist to form
full   heavy drops that
gather at the tips   of scimitar leaves.

Pattern on a Pavement

The pavement like an etched plate
ready for printing
has been inked this morning
with yellow ink
and the plate wiped clean
with a rag of wind
leaving the incised lines
loaded
ready for an impression.
The ink is Bottlebrush stamens
from the ornamental trees,
the design
a pattern of horizontals
between the segments of paving,
and the imprint of dogs' paws,
and a heart with initials in it.

The Beach

The beach is a quarter of golden fruit,
a soft ripe melon
sliced to a half-moon curve,
having a thick green rind
of jungle growth;
and the sea devours it
with its sharp,
sharp white teeth.

Shell-collecting

Yesterday while sifting shell-
debris in a rock pool and
sieving it through my fingers
carefully so as not to
disturb the sandy sediment
and silt and wait for it to settle
I must have pulled the bedclothes
from a small brown octopus
who stared at me a moment with I swear
surprise suddenly extended
the tip of a tentacle
and pulled back over his head
his multicoloured shellpiece
patchwork quilt.

Entente Cordiale

Alone on the beach
early this morning
collecting shells
searching along the line of debris
left by the last high tide
stooping and picking
stooping and picking
a pigeon joined me
bobbing and pecking
bobbing and pecking.

The Dam

Away, across, and over, through
miles of yellow saffron-thistle
quietly smoking down, thistledown
in the distance

to the dam
in the south-east corner
to the right
of the wheat-paddock

where, under the paperbarks
the brown-wooled sheep are
lumped like still
stones.

Lake Monger

On Lake Monger a black swan
makes of its neck an interrogation-mark
punctuating a sentence of ducks.

Vapour Trail

It was flying
at some tremendous height —

slow, dawdling almost
across the empty sky

so minute,
remote,

I could hear nothing,
see no silver glint

no tiny pin-point
burrowing cause of it —

only a vapour trail,
a thin, straight

thread
of white

dust
behind a vehicle on

the sky road
overhead.

Thunderstorm

The summer sky has permitted
the temper tantrum of a violent
thunderstorm which is now a disc
of black cloud drifting north west
diminishing, a scarf almost
of remorse trailing from it

It has left the parched
earth the gift of sheets of
surface water everywhere
in which the sky is reflected

A bird with match-stick thin
legs treads the surprising water
probing, a flock of
fly-size birds is in a frenzy
and all the frogs in the
world have reincarnated
and sing its praises
and the sweet world reeks of ozone.

Welshpool Road

In the distant hills
a flicker of summer lightning

Someone is working overtime tonight
in the welding shop.

Smoke on the Plains

I can follow with my eyes a scarf of haze
fifteen miles back into the hills
from the plains, where someone started a blaze
this morning of newly-cut gorse.

Tonight it twinkles like a window
winking back the setting sun.
It seems an old legend recurs
continually in the soul,

and here is yet another variation.
And so I feel I want to go and take
a hand in what they make.

Burning Off

Don't heed them. Those fires are tame
burning over the hill. The tethered dogs
lie with chain slack, sleeping. The smoke
is invisible, it is something in the air
makes all day's colours sombre, a fragrance,
subtle, nameless. And you may have noticed
the early stars are not of the purest water
and do not twinkle. The grass, the grass is dry,
the roof metal shines like steel
under a paring of moon. Like a procession
of torchbearers going on some pilgrimage,
the lines of flame on the hilltop.
Leave the door open. Come inside.
The night grows cold. Light the lamp.

Looking for Shells

One quiet summer Sunday evening
when I was looking for shells

along a beach from which
the crowd was beginning to go

walking along the water's edge
looking down at my toes

stopping sometimes and stooping
to pick something up

to examine closely
and put it down again

a small boy, came running down
from the dry sand

and enquired
Mister have you lost something?

Night Fishing

The harbour is so calm tonight
the piles of the wharf are motionless

not a creak or groan
from the wooden decking

we sit holding our lines
sit holding the thread

of nylon speaking if we must
in whispers

the harbour is so calm
tonight we start

when a small fish breaks the surface
for a second

flashing a
silver moonflash on its scales.

Mini Poem from a Pillow

Full moon.

Heron on a pine-branch.

Perfect silhouette

if only heron

or moon

would move over a bit.

Full Moon

The full moon
poking about in the dark under the house
came up over the edge of the verandah
with a whisp of sooty cobweb on his face.

Candle

My candle is a kindly light, my candle
burns with a companionable flame.
All by myself in my room at night

a single candlepower to give me light
and keep me warm.
My candle is a golden lily

that flowers on a long white stem.
My candle is a tongue that softly
licks the black fur of my room.

Derelict House

As if to save others the trouble
a kind of winter-flowering honeysuckle
is pulling itself over
an old wooden house
like a green dust-cover.

Kumara

This sweet-potato is baked unevenly,
one end is nicely cooked,
the other underdone.

A wise man says nothing.
He eats both ends together.

Tractor

Dragging an iron rake
the tractor wallows
across the ocean of the paddock
with a fine excitement of gulls
in its wake.

It has two large paddle wheels,
a funnel, with smoke;
and the captain is on the bridge.
Having cast off a couple
of moments ago,
he sets a course for the opposite hedge.

Haystacks and Limestone

Sheep nibble at
this outcrop of rock
made of hay,

and up against the sky
there are the shapes again
in limestone
crags and along the

corridors of eternity
hurry wind-shepherds
droving cloud-sheep that nibble

holes, caverns, pockets.

Windmill

The windmill by the water-tank
with his see-through face
and base of latticed iron bars
reminds me of a fisherman
standing ankle-deep in the shallows
of a lake full of minnows
featureless horizon to horizon –
who suddenly enmeshes the water
with a throwing-net of galahs.

Lighthouses

Lighthouses mark capes, headlands,
shoals and cliffs and reefs,
sometimes standing well back inland
out of touch with the dangers they mark
or high on a cliff-top, aloof.

Lighthouses on different maps
are indicated in different ways.
This one uses a star,
a circle, a dot at the centre;
and this a rod with radiating rays.

I always seem to come upon lighthouses from
    the rear
these days, from the landside. From here
they belong more to the sea than the land.

A lighthouse stands and looks at the sea.
If I tap it on the shoulder
it doesn't turn round.

It's in a trance, of sorts,
hypnotised by the sea
that passes a hand in front of its eyes,
to and fro,
with slow and somnolent gestures.

Were I a sailor, or given to sailing,
a lighthouse would belong to the land.
It would not be looking at me
or looking for me,
it would simply be a quiet, white,
impersonal thing, a remote warning,
or a rhythmical on-and-off light.

I'd see the long white finger going round,
if it were night
and the night were clear,
right round the horizon,
and I would remark
on the interminable time it seems to take
to make one revolution of its spoke.

I went with my father once
up the spiral stairs inside a lighthouse.

We knocked on the door and a man opened it.
The keeper wore a blue uniform
with polished brass buttons.

Each room was a cell with round walls
one on top of the other
like cells in a plant stem
rooms with walls of whitewashed stone
with lots of burnished copper and brass,
buckets, ropes and lanterns
all on hooks and shelves,
gleaming, smelling of scrubbing and cleanness.

One was a kitchen. One was a sleeping room
with beds in a room without corners.
And right at the top
was an enormous diamond
with multiple facets
and the smallest, most ridiculously small
lantern at the heart of it.

Beacon fires in black iron baskets,
flaming and smoking
on rocky promontories
were the forerunners of lighthouses.

I'd say, if I were a sailor
at sea then

There are people there and it comforts me.
Some lighthouses are white towers
rising from a cluster of buildings
somewhat remotely reminding me
of a medieval cathedral far away,
oasis of safety, monument of peace.

Others, especially now,
now that the door at the base
is always shut
and hasn't a handle,
only an empty black keyhole,
are solitary pillars of white stone
without a friend in the world
and there's no one inside.
And fine or storm, calm or rough,
night turns the light on
and the day turns off.

Cyclone

The first rain in months
drops
drops
splash on the roadway
from a clear blue sky
overhead

Footprints of the Spirit Dog

spatter on the asphalt
of the desert road
in the ominous stillness
in the looming darkness

They print their pawmarks
on the dry road
on the windscreen dust

From the wide desert
the kangaroos come out
bend down on their huge haunches
go down on their hands
to
to lap the road
to lap the drops

lick from the road
the raindrops

the first rain.

The Ghost of MacKenzie's Dog

Some have said that sometime
far out under the night
they discern strange movement among the sheep
and swear they hear a bark,
though when the dogs are tallied no animal
is left to account for it.
Sheep scattered in the dark
call to each other, they disperse
but keep in touch, their wandering
is no more haphazard than the stars'
scattered in the heaven, each
knows where all the others are.
So that when the calling of sheep
sounds in unison and faintly
one hears the patter of their feet
as they file head to tail,

and numbers are gathered in a cluster, shaped,
rounded, herded, pressed toward a
gate and those along the ridge
trot in ghostly silhouette – surely
a dog is out there making a muster?
'Run out, Jack, and call the animal in!'
But all the movement has stopped, the sheep
are calmly grazing
under the moon and the white
stars and the dog has gone.

Can You Stand Still Enough ...?

Can you stand
still enough to hold

and fix one flawless
liquid jewel blazing

blue-green, crimson, gold
on a leaf-tip for a second;

so motionless
your head does not rock

even that fraction
the blood's arterial pulsing makes it?

Absolutely critical
is the angle

if you would crystallise
for a moment

a single water-diamond
in the wattle.

Derelict Hut

Why do they put pennies
on a dead man's eyes?
It is to close the windows securely
for when the soul flies
eyes have a look no man should see.
For this same reason the eyes
of this hut are nailed
with boards, it seems to me.

Full Moon (1)

Full moon is moving
across the sky tonight
in and out behind
and through the clouds

It is a pearl shell
traded across the land
passed swiftly
silently from hand to hand.

Index of First Lines

A

A flight of white pigeons 12
After the rain 55
A golden stallion with honey-coloured
    mane 37
A grey heron in the twilight 14
A Kangaroo Paw 58
All up the hillside 66
Alone on the beach 77
A quickly drying tail 46
As if to save others the trouble 91
A single cloud over the city 72
Away, across, and over, through 78
A yellow lizard 45

B

Bellbirds chiming in the bush 3
Birds 18
Brown out of the brown tussock a
    darker brown 42

C

Can you stand 104
Clusters of Paperbark trees 62
Cones exploding sharply in the heat? . . . 65

D

Don't heed them. Those fires are tame 85
Down there on the dark rock sharp to
    the foot 29
Dragging an iron rake 93

E

Eaglehawk is like a leaf in the air 6

F

Fire can't take me by the throat 54
First come the blunt 53
Fourteen white-fronted shags 4
From a machine-gun nest 16
Full moon 88
Full moon is moving 106

H

He comes loping across the flat from the
    direction of 40
Here on the side of a hill 73
High above the screen 5

I

I can follow with my eyes a scarf of haze 84
If the shark is my enemy 34
If you were 32
I'm looking forward to spring again
    already 63
Injured, it walked on my finger 48
In the distant hills 83
In this forty-degree heat 24
It saddens me to see the fallen trees 60
It was flying 80
I wonder whether the magpie 17

J

Jellyfish are sea bells 31

K

Kneel and feel with your hands 50

L

Leaves are cold green 67
Lighthouses mark capes, headlands 96

M

Magpies aren't greedy 8
My candle is a kindly light, my candle 90

N

Not for the spider 26
Now the cyclorama of night is softly 20

O

One obstinate gull 10
One quiet summer Sunday evening 86
On Lake Monger a black swan 79

S

Sheep nibble at 94
She said what kind of bird is that 25
Some have said that sometime 102
Someone is flying balloons 30

T

The beach is a quarter of golden fruit 75
The enormous cumulus 64
The first rain in months 100
The flock of pigeons 11
The full moon 89
The harbour is so calm tonight 87
The main reason why dogs 38

The pavement like an etched plate 74
The summer sky has permitted 82
There are about fifty of them 13
The tall slender gum 61
The way the Fly-catcher 3
The windmill by the water-tank 95
They had all time in front of them 56
This sweet-potato is baked unevenly 92
Trees are the world's lungs, gills 59
Trigger-plants have their hammers pulled
    back 57

U

Under the sea, deep 36

W

Wading into the warm sea 71
Whenever I peep 23
When I switched on the bar-light 27
Why do sand crabs witlessly 28
Why do they put pennies 105
With a single caw 5
Wouldn't you think the salmon 33

Y

Yes, I'll stop for a snake 44
Yesterday while sifting shell- 76

A short account of the life and work of William Hart-Smith appears in Brian Dibble's article, 'He will be lonely in heaven' which was published in *Southern Review*, November 1990.